Bible S

A DVD-based study series
Study Guide

ISAIAH 53

The Mysterious Prophecy

A DVD-based study series
Study Guide

ISAIAH 53

The Mysterious Prophecy

Nine Lessons for Group Exploration

DISCOVERY HOUSE

P U B L I S H E R S ®

Feeding the Soul with the Word of God

**The DayLight Bible Studies are based on programs produced by
Day of Discovery, a Bible-teaching TV series of RBC Ministries.**

© 2012 by Discovery House Publishers

Discovery House Publishers is affiliated with RBC Ministries,
Grand Rapids, Michigan.

Requests for permission to quote from this book should be directed to:

Permissions Department
Discovery House Publishers
P.O. Box 3566
Grand Rapids, MI 49501
Or contact us by e-mail at permissionsdept@dhp.org

Study questions by Andrew Sloan
Interior design by Sherri L. Hoffman
Cover design by Jeremy Culp
Cover photo by iStockphoto

ISBN: 978-1-57293-761-1

Printed in the United States of America
First Printing 2012

CONTENTS

INTRODUCTION

A Matter of Perspective

How can two people read the same document and come away with diametrically opposed ideas about what that document means? You would think that simple words on paper would be interpreted similarly by reasonably intelligent people, but we know through life experiences that shades of meaning and opposing philosophies color the process of understanding the written word.

Think, for instance, of the U.S. Constitution, one of the most hallowed documents in human history. On the surface, it seems to be a rather straightforward piece of writing. The framers of it were not trying to be tricky or sly—they simply wanted to codify the foundation of the United States' government as they felt in their wisdom that it should be constituted and put into practice.

But from the time that parchment was first unscrolled and read, it has been examined and re-read and analyzed for its meanings and interpretations. From the beginning of U.S. history, a team of nine people has been charged with interpreting this document in regard to the laws and rulings and standards of the land. And we are all aware of the innumerable controversies that have brewed over the past 225-plus years as the meaning of the Constitution has been debated.

For a much more significant segment of mankind's history, another document has been discussed and debated: the Bible. And in particular, one specific part of that document has come to represent a kind of demarcation line between two religions: Christianity and Judaism. At the crux of this "line in the sand" is the book of Isaiah, chapter 53.

As with two sides in a political debate discussing a portion of the Constitution, people of the Christian faith and people of the Jewish faith have hotly contested the meaning of Isaiah 53. One may read in that passage the story of the servant Israel, a nation that has often been mistreated and misused as the passage describes. And the other may read in those same words the story of an individual, a Man who was mistreated and abused as He gave himself as the Messiah—the Savior—of the world.

What would it take to examine that passage and come to a definitive, trustworthy decision about the servant of Isaiah 53? Four scholars attempted to do this by using their training and their background to decipher the meaning of the prophet's words. Adding to the perspective of three of these men is the fact that they grew up on one side of this issue and changed their view along the way; three of them are Jewish by birth. Two of these men grew up in homes where they were taught that the Man in the passage could not possibly be Jesus.

It's a fascinating study as they move through the evidences they have found to support the assertion that Isaiah 53 is about Messiah Jesus. Along the way, they also examine the points made by those who say this portion of Scripture cannot be tied in any way to Him.

You'll be challenged in your thinking and entertained from time to time with the stories these men tell about their youth and their discoveries regarding this vital portion of Scripture as they examine the mysterious prophecy of Isaiah 53. In the end, it comes down to more than a matter of perspective—it is a matter of eternal life and death.

—Dave Branon
Editor

The Mysterious Prophecy of Isaiah 53

DAYLIGHT PREVIEW

Testing the Prophecy

"All prophecies are tested by time." So ends the documentary that accompanies this lesson. Time—thousands of years of it—has passed since the prophet Isaiah sat before his scroll and wrote down the words, the God-breathed words, of his book. Toward the end of Isaiah's writings, he was inspired to write of a servant who would one day suffer for Israel and for the world. The identity of that servant is still being tested and contested these many millennia later. Can we in the twenty-first century say with certainty who the prophet was referring to in Isaiah 52:13–Isaiah 53:12? Has the testing of time revealed to us who was "crushed for our iniquities" and by whose "wounds we are healed"? Is this Jesus? Can we know for sure that Isaiah of old was speaking about a Messiah born in Bethlehem? Or was the penman speaking of Israel as he wrote of a suffering servant? Which of these two possibilities has passed the test of time?

FINDING DAYLIGHT

Experience the Video

The Day of Discovery television team, as an introduction to the panel discussion that is to follow, prepared a documentary that takes an overall look at the controversy surrounding this vital chapter of the Bible. *The Mysterious Prophecy of Isaiah 53* presents the main discussion points that relate to Isaiah 53 and how it is interpreted by two major religions: Judaism and

Christianity. Feel free to jot down Video Notes as you watch the documentary. Use the space below for those notes.

──────────── VIDEO NOTES ────────────

The vision of Isaiah

The different parts of the vision

The mystery of "my servant"

The Jewish view

Who is the suffering servant?

Suggestions of the rabbis   2 different Messiah say

The Community Rule

Dead Sea Scrolls and Isaiah   *discovery 19 47 + 56*
The greatest discovery ever made   *21 scrolls of Isaiah*
From the Essenes a sect of Judaism — Is. was the favorite - the key prophet

First-century Jews

Shrine of the Book   *Israel Museum   24' scroll*

Jesus and the gospels - *a new era w/in Judaism (not a new relig.)*
✱   *Only 1 place (Lk 4) when Jesus read from the Scr.*

Ethiopian Treasurer + Philip
Quoting from Isaiah

Those close to Jesus

Jesus' death
crushed for our iniquities
death incl. piercing
All we like sheep have gone astray — he is our substitution

The servant: Jesus or Israel? - *described as a person*
Jews read 11th c. BC commentaries who saw the servant as the Nation

Jesus connects himself w. the servant of Is 53

Jesus spoke of the future Kingdom

All prophecies are tested by time

Mt 5:17

WALKING IN THE DAYLIGHT

Discussion Time

DISCOVER GOD'S WORD

Discussion Questions

1. How does this documentary give you reason to view Isaiah 53 in a different way?

2. What seems to be the key question that needs to be answered as you consider the differing ways Judaism and Christianity view this passage? Consider Isaiah 41:9 and Isaiah 52:13.

3. How is it possible these two groups—who both love Old Testament Scripture—see the answer to this question so differently?

4. What great archaeological discovery re-ignited this argument in the mid-1900s? What do you know about the Dead Sea Scrolls other than what the documentary revealed? Has anyone visited an exhibit of its artifacts?

5. Discuss the suggestion given that what Jesus and His disciples were doing was not starting a new religion but instead anticipating changes in Judaism.

6. A couple of New Testament passages—Luke 4:18-21 and Acts 8:26-35—suggest how important Isaiah was to people in Jesus' day. In what way was this true?

7. According to Michael Rydelnik, what are some ways Jesus' life and death are revealed in Isaiah 53?

8. According to Michael Brown, Jewish scholars going back hundreds of years have exposed a different interpretation of Isaiah 53. What does their reading of it say will happen regarding salvation of Gentiles?

9. How important does it seem that, as is mentioned in the documentary, Jesus linked himself not just to Isaiah but to all of Judaism?

DAYLIGHT ON PRAYER

Spending Time with God

As you contemplate the importance of a right understanding of Scripture, ask God for clarity as you open His Word. Pray for the Holy Spirit to reveal to each of you His truth through Scripture to help you know how to live each day for His glory.

DAYLIGHT AHEAD

A visit to Israel and a visit with four biblical scholars introduce this discussion of Isaiah 53 by giving us an overview of the Bible's big picture: There is a corporate need because "all of us" have failed, and we need someone to take our guilt so we can be reconciled to God. But who is this one? Who is the "servant" of Isaiah 53? That is the issue these scholars begin to explore in Session 2.

The Essence of the Bible Story

DAYLIGHT PREVIEW

A Journey to the Future

In the middle of the stories of an ancient people who struggled to obey God appears a section of Scripture that some people say takes the reader out of that time and transports him or her hundreds of years into the future. That section, which is found in chapters 52 and 53 of the book of Isaiah, is a source of controversy and heated discussion regarding biblical interpretation. As a new discussion of this passage gets underway, four scholars who are well-versed in biblical studies begin by explaining the big picture of the Bible: What is the essence of this long book in which this futuristic story found in Isaiah 53 resides?

COME TOGETHER

Icebreaker Questions

1. These videos are based in Israel, the land of the Bible. Have you ever visited Israel? If so, what did you enjoy the most?

2. The focus of this study is the "servant" of Isaiah 53. In what sense did you most feel like a servant when you were growing up?

3. Who was your hero as a child? Have you ever had a hero who wasn't the kind of person who would likely be considered powerful or attractive, but maintained a character or presence that was magnetic?

FINDING DAYLIGHT

Experience the Video

Feel free to jot down Video Notes as you watch the presentation. Use the space below for those notes.

2. The Mystery of Deliverance

―――――― VIDEO NOTES ――――――

All prophecy is tested by time.

Michael Rydelnik's introduction

This chap is going where we haven't been before

This chap can change your life – a journey into the future

The Bible has 1 thread   Is 53 is the Bible in a nutshell – a microcosm

1 big story

The other scholars *What is the main idea of the Bible – the big story*

Walter Kaiser *There is a design to reconnect back with God*

Is 53:6 all of us have sinned fallen short

The surprise – weak, not powerful – not the one we would expect – not powerful figure

Michael Brown

Darrell Bock

What's the big story?

What's the main idea of Isaiah 53? *That an innocent one takes upon his shoulder the sin & guilt of the whole world*

53:6 All we like sheep have gone astray

What do we need to know? *- ask who the Servant is - an individual or a group or a nation*

Who is he? *what will he do - will he die*
" " rise from death

Sacrificial language

The suffering and rejection of Isaiah 53 *an important part of the picture*
God exalts the humble, who depends on Him.

The M.
Through his suffering he is exalted

Suffering leads to exaltation and success
The Servant is treated like a leper - disconnected from humanity
language that He will be exalted 52:13 - 53:12 brackets
My servant will have success

Dr. Rydelnik's summary *- the message of the Bible is that all people are strayed from God - Dad will send his servant to bring us back to him.*

WALKING IN THE DAYLIGHT

Discussion Time

——————— DISCOVER GOD'S WORD ———————
Discussion/Application Questions

1. To what extent have you studied the Jewish Scriptures, or Old Testament, in general, and the book of Isaiah in particular?

2. How familiar are you with Isaiah 53 (actually Isaiah 52:13 to 53:12) and its presentation of the rather mysterious "suffering servant"?

3. Read Isaiah 52:13 to 53:12.

   What are your first impressions of this passage? What stands out to you?

4. Michael Rydelnik asserts that the prophecy of Isaiah 53 reveals the essence of the story of the Bible. Darrell Bock adds that the story of the Bible is that God's design for our relationship with Him has been damaged, but He has made a way for us to reconnect with Him.

   a. What was God's original design for our relationship with Him? How do we know that?

   b. How was that relationship damaged? How do we know that?

   c. How do we get reconnected to God?

5. Michael Brown points to the significance of Isaiah 53:6 both starting and ending with how "all of us" have fallen short and failed. The apostle Paul echoed this point when he wrote, "All have sinned and fall short of the glory of God" (Romans 3:23).

How countercultural, or "politically incorrect," is it to claim that all people are sinners?

6. Isaiah 53:6 also contends that this one central figure, the suffering servant, has taken the guilt of all of us so we can be reconciled to God.

How does that strike you: Logical and legitimate? Mysterious and mystical? Too good to be true? Too amazing to be anything but God?

7. How do you feel about viewing the Messiah, as Dr. Bock notes, in terms of a leper—i.e., a person, in the context of Judaism, who was banished from functioning in society?

──────────── BRINGING IT HOME ────────────

1. As Darrell Bock says, this amazing figure of Isaiah 53 is not at all the powerful figure that you would think, and yet out of that weakness, or seeming weakness, comes the delivery of the power of God.

How have you seen God at work in the midst of and through your weakness?

2. What do you hope to gain from this study and from spending time with this group?

DAYLIGHT ON PRAYER

Spending Time with God

1. Do you have any questions or struggles in your relationship with God that you would like your group to pray with you about?

2. Do you have any other prayer requests to share with the group?

DAYLIGHT AHEAD

A servant is coming. But who is that servant? First, there has to be an agreement about how to interpret Isaiah 53. But who makes that decision? Can it be interpreted by rabbis using their commentaries to see Israel as the servant? Or does there have to be a different interpretation? As the discussion continues, those are questions that are being answered by scholars who have spent countless hours examining this issue.

What Is Isaiah 53 About?

DAYLIGHT PREVIEW

Curveballs and Rabbis

How is Isaiah 53 to be interpreted, and whose job is it to give it meaning? Scholars Michael Rydelnik, Michael Brown, Darrell Bock, and Walter Kaiser pick up their discussion of this passage by examining the ways it can be interpreted. Dr. Bock uses a baseball analogy to suggest that some explanations of the chapter come at the interpreter like a curveball that can cause confusion. Dr. Brown suggests that Jewish rabbis have interpretations informed by hundreds of years of scholarship. The question remains, then: Who knows how to rightly explain who the servant is in this passage?

——— COME TOGETHER ———

Icebreaker Questions

1. Michael Brown talks about the importance of communication and the fact that the writers of Scripture wrote to communicate God's will and God's heart to His people. How would you describe the level and quality of communication in the home you grew up in?

2. Dr. Brown notes that when an athlete wins a gold medal, his or her country wins a gold medal. How excited, and patriotic, do you get when it's time for the Olympics?

3. Dr. Brown also recounts how, as a young person, he interacted for hours and hours with kindly ultra-Orthodox Jewish rabbis who studied day and night. What subject or activity has captivated you for hours on end?

3. What is Is 53 about

FINDING DAYLIGHT

Experience the Video

All prophecies are testified

Feel free to jot down Video Notes as you watch the presentation. Use the space below for those notes.

Graphic details
miraculously lifted up **VIDEO NOTES**

Isaiah's prediction — *a servant will come to lead us back to God*

Walter Kaiser: Bible interpretation

Michael Brown: Communication

Darrell Bock's curveball illustration — *don't be caught off*

Columbus

A rabbi's reading of Isaiah 53

Using commentaries of the 11th C BC — the nation

Get the full picture — Israel as servant
the nation has failed

Is 41 Israel — after Ch 48 it is an individual — (it doesn't fit the nation)

Mary "treasured these things"

It is a prediction
It describes a delivering figure
When Jesus comes — we see the connection
700 yrs before Christ
Jesus is my sin-bearer

The servant fulfills the nation's purpose

Understanding the context and the backdrop

Is prior knowledge needed?

The details of the passage: Like the New Testament

The delivering figure: Three characteristics

Date of authorship of the book   *700 BC or (500 BC for 3rd Isaiah)*

Personal impact of the passage

A timeless question   *Who has believed our report?*

WALKING IN THE DAYLIGHT

Discussion Time

—————————— DISCOVER GOD'S WORD ——————

Discussion/Application Questions

1. **Michael Rydelnik notes that a lot of people say, "Oh, the Bible means whatever you want it to mean."**

   How would you respond to that charge? Discuss how damaging that way of thinking can be.

2. **What do you think of Darrell Bock's "curveball" warning about getting caught off balance and being forced to make a choice about what the text means that the text itself is not asking us to make?**

3. Michael Brown says the interpretation of traditional Judaism is that the servant in Isaiah 53 is Israel, and Isaiah is speaking of the suffering of the Jewish people, or the righteous remnant, as they are scattered around the world and suffer through the centuries—with the result that through this suffering healing somehow comes to the world.

   a. How familiar are you with that interpretation?

   b. Do you agree with Dr. Brown's conclusion that this interpretation just doesn't work? Why?

4. What does Dr. Brown mean when he says that the servant is the ideal one, the ideal Jew who actually accomplishes Israel's mission?

5. The immediate context of Isaiah 52:13–53:12 is Isaiah's prophetic future description of the Jewish people coming out of the exile in Babylon. Read Isaiah 52:1–12.

   How do you suppose the Israelites, who were exiled in Babylon many years after Isaiah proclaimed these words, felt as they read them?

6. Dr. Brown states, "It's against that backdrop [of Isaiah 52:1–12] that many of the wonderful promises, the wonderful prophecies, were given of how God will bring the Redeemer and how God will bring our people back to Him. Now there's a greater exile that we'll be delivered from."

What is that greater exile that we'll be delivered from?

7. How is the amazing predictive quality of the passage affected even more by the fact that Isaiah is typically dated about 700 years before Jesus (or by some scholars who are skeptical of that dating, still 500 years before the time of Jesus)?

————— BRINGING IT HOME —————

Michael Brown recounts how reading Isaiah 53 changed his life while he was young. "With all my heart I wanted to please God. I remember lying down on my face in my bedroom, and I said, 'God, I've got to follow you as a Jew wherever the truth leads. If it means leaving all my friends and everyone that I've gotten to know who believes in Jesus and living the life of a traditional Jew, I will follow you. And if it means following Jesus, if what I believe is true, I will follow you. And I don't care if the Jewish community rejects me. I have to be loyal to you as a Jew.'"

To what extent can you relate to seeking God like that and inviting Him to call you to account and to faithfulness?

DAYLIGHT ON PRAYER

Spending Time with God

1. How can the group support you in prayer as you seek to know God and be faithful to Him?

2. What other prayer requests would you like to share with your group?

DAYLIGHT AHEAD

A man on a mission. That's one way to look at the servant presented in Isaiah 53. Could that person—that man—be found in this chapter? Or is He just the figment of the imagination of Christians—as Michael Rydelnik was told as a young child? The panel of scholars examine this and other possible ways Isaiah 53 can be interpreted.

God's Faithful, Exalted Servant

DAYLIGHT PREVIEW

On a Mission

No one would argue that Isaiah 53 is about a servant. The text makes that clear, and it seems that this servant is on a mission. But who is this servant—this faithful, exalted servant? Is it, as Michael Rydelnik was taught as a boy, the people or the nation of Israel? Is it an Old Testament figure such as Moses? Or is it, as the scholars who are discussing Isaiah 53 in this study suggest, one person: Jesus Christ? Is there evidence enough to know who this servant on a mission really is? This is the question Michael Brown, Walter Kaiser, and Darrell Bock discuss in this session.

COME TOGETHER

Icebreaker Questions

1. Michael Rydelnik begins this session by saying, "I was raised in a traditional Jewish home. That's why I love being here in Israel. Every time I come here, it's like coming home." What place seems to you like a second home?

2. The discussion in this session turns toward the servant in Isaiah 53 as being the "perfect Israel." On a scale of 1 (naughty) to 10 (nice), how close were you to being a "perfect" child?

3. Walter Kaiser points out that the role and title of "servant" can be one of honor, a designation for a person who is deputized for a very special work. Who is someone you know who stands out as a great example of a true and noble servant?

FINDING DAYLIGHT

Experience the Video

Feel free to jot down Video Notes as you watch the presentation. Use the space below for those notes.

──────────────VIDEO NOTES──────────────

Michael Rydelnik's story

How has Isaiah 53 been interpreted?

a. In early Judaism: Some references to Messiah

b. Suffering Messiah, Moses

c. A righteous group within the nation

d. The nation of Israel

e. Blood-letting

Big Three Jewish interpreters

Dealing with the word *servant*

Israel as servant

The servant carries out a mission

Discussion Time

DISCOVER GOD'S WORD

Discussion/Application Questions

1. In the history of Judaism, there have been many interpretations of the servant in Isaiah 52:13–53:12: a highly exalted Messiah, a suffering Messiah, Moses, the nation of Israel, or a righteous group within the nation.

   What evidence do you see for these various interpretations?

2. The first time the book of Isaiah mentions the concept of God's servant is in Isaiah 41:8. Read Isaiah 41:8–14. (Note: Jacob was the son of Isaac, the son of Abraham, and the father of the twelve sons whose descendants became the twelve tribes of Israel. God gave Jacob the name Israel, and both "Israel" and "Jacob" became synonymous with the nation.)

   a. What indicators are there that this passage refers to the nation of Israel?

   b. What promises does the Lord give the people?

3. **Now read Isaiah 42:18–22, another passage that refers to the Lord's servant.**

   a. What indicators are there that this passage refers to the nation of Israel?

   b. How well have the people fulfilled their calling?

   c. Since both this passage and Isaiah 41:8–14 seem to refer to the nation of Israel, how can we reconcile the stark difference in tone?

4. **Now read Isaiah 49:1–7, which is one of the so-called "servant songs" in the book of Isaiah.**

   How does the fact that verse 5 states that the servant has a mission *to* Israel support Walter Kaiser's assertion that although Israel has always had a servant role, in Isaiah 49 the identity of the servant switches to an individual who is that servant—the perfect Israel?

5. **What are the implications of the fact that the Jewish Scriptures refer to Moses, David, and Joshua as "the servant of the Lord"?**

6. When God called Abraham, He promised to bless all the peoples of the earth through Abraham and his offspring (Genesis 12:2–3). What does that tell us about the mission of Israel in general and of the servant of Isaiah 53 in particular?

—————————— BRINGING IT HOME ——————————

Michael Brown states that the servant has the mission of making God known, and Isaiah 52:13–53:12 expresses how the servant would enter into our suffering and bring us back to God. The servant of the Lord bridges the gap caused by our sins and makes a way where God can reach out to us in our need and forgive our sins.

How much can you relate to a sense of appreciation for God's servant, the Messiah, entering into your suffering in order to bring you back to God and forgive your sins?

DAYLIGHT ON PRAYER

Spending Time with God

1. In what area of your life or in what way would you like God to enter into your suffering or challenges?

2. What concerns for yourself, others, or world events would you like the group to pray with you about?

DAYLIGHT AHEAD

"It can't be Jesus." That quote from a book Michael Rydelnik read presents an interesting jumping off point for the continuing discussion of who Isaiah 53 is talking about. It seems that there are certain traits mentioned in Isaiah 53 that some say prove the description cannot be about Jesus. In order to properly answer that suggestion, the panel digs into Isaiah 53 to look at it in a fresh, unbiased way to see exactly what it says. That, they suggest, should provide the answer to who this chapter is talking about.

Can This *Really* Be Jesus?

DAYLIGHT PREVIEW

Examining the Clues

How do people with preconceived notions about something take an unbiased look at an important issue? They do so by revisiting the facts and analyzing them as honestly as possible. That's what the panel of Michael Brown, Darrell Bock, Walter Kaiser, and moderater Michael Rydelnik try to do in this session. By looking at the details of the language as it relates to the servant of Isaiah 53, they try to figure out who the passage is talking about: The references to an individual. The singular personal pronouns. The voice of the narrator. The clues begin to add up as the discussion continues.

—————— COME TOGETHER ——————

Icebreaker Questions

1. Isaiah 53:2 talks about the servant's lowly upbringing. Who do you admire for what they've accomplished in spite of their lowly upbringing?

2. The servant grew up as an ordinary person. Who was (or is) your favorite ordinary-person-turned-superhero in the comic book/movie genre?

3. Jesus never defended himself against the accusations made against Him. How true was that of you when you were growing up and you were accused by a sibling, playmate, or classmate?

FINDING DAYLIGHT

Experience the Video

Feel free to jot down Video Notes as you watch the presentation. Use the space below for those notes.

────────────── **VIDEO NOTES** ──────────────

Identifying the servant

Why some say the servant can't be Jesus

An individual or a group?

The exaltation of Jesus

The idea of resurrection

So what?

There is a message here

What do we do with our sins?

Restoration and reconnection

Michael Rydelnik and Jesus

WALKING IN THE DAYLIGHT

Discussion Time

DISCOVER GOD'S WORD

Discussion/Application Questions

1. How convincing do you find the argument, based on Isaiah 53:10, that the servant can't be Jesus because Jesus had no descendants (i.e., "seed" or "offspring")?

2. What is the significance of the fact that there is a sect of ultra-Orthodox Jews, based in Crown Heights, Brooklyn, that interprets Isaiah 53 with reference to its leader, the grand rabbi of the Lubavitch, even though he and his wife had no children?

3. As Michael Brown details, how does the language of Isaiah 52:13–53:12 seem much more relevant to an individual rather than to Israel or a group within Israel?

4. The New Testament demonstrates how Jesus fulfilled Isaiah 53. Read Mark 15:1–5.

   Why do you think Jesus didn't defend himself? Was it simply to fulfill prophecies like Isaiah 53:7?

5. How is the idea of the servant's resurrection included in Isaiah 52:13–53:12?

6. Michael Rydelnik asks this question: "If God predicted the coming of the servant over 700 years before Jesus, why is that so significant?" How would you answer that question? What is the message here?

7. Darrell Bock mentions the Jewish expression *L'chaim*—"To life." And then he states, "I think we sometimes sell the gospel short in how we share it as Christians, because we make it all about fixing sin or avoiding hell or avoiding a bad thing."

   a. How is Isaiah 52:13–53:12 ultimately about life and restoration?

   b. What does Dr. Bock mean when he says that when you reconnect to God, you reconnect to the way you were designed to live?

BRINGING IT HOME

Isaiah 53:6 says, "All we, like sheep, have gone astray." Reflecting on that statement, Michael Brown observes, "The more religious and spiritual a person is, the more he tends to recognize how rotten he can be."

How much can you relate to that principle?

DAYLIGHT ON PRAYER

Spending Time with God

1. How do you feel about your level of vulnerability and communication with God? How can the group pray for you in that regard?

2. Do you have any other prayer requests to share with the group?

DAYLIGHT AHEAD

So, what was the servant who has been discussed so far in this study supposed to do? He was slated for sacrifice. Everyone who knew the Old Testament knew about the sacrificial system. But how does Isaiah 53 and this servant relate to that system? This is the direction the panel of Bible scholars takes next as they examine Isaiah's mention of such things as sprinkling and substitutionary atonement. Are there any clues in the text to suggest who is responsible for those things happening? Session 6 helps answer these questions.

A Lesson in Atonement

DAYLIGHT PREVIEW

Pictures from the Torah

The images presented in Isaiah 53 would not have been new to the original readers of this section of the book. They would have known what the prophet was talking about when he spoke of sins being borne by another; they would have recalled the sacrificial system that was recorded in the first five books of the Old Testament—the Torah. But how did all of that relate to the subject of this section? Does the discussion of the sacrificial system help explain who it is Isaiah 53 is describing?

——————— COME TOGETHER ———————

Icebreaker Questions

1. This session begins with a discussion of animal sacrifices. What is one of the greatest "sacrifices" you've ever made?

2. One specific offering that is addressed is the guilt offering, which a person would offer after committing certain sins and which was accompanied by some form of restitution. As a kid, how quick were you to accept guilt when you did wrong? How did you feel about making restitution?

3. This session ends on a note of grace. Aside from being a recipient of God's grace, when have you been the beneficiary of positive treatment you didn't deserve?

FINDING DAYLIGHT

Experience the Video

Feel free to jot down Video Notes as you watch the presentation. Use the space below for those notes.

————————— VIDEO NOTES —————————

The temple of Jerusalem

The sacrifice

Images of sacrifice: Bearing sin, sprinkling

A human, not an animal, as the sacrifice

Day of Atonement

Substitutionary atonement

Perfect sacrifice: Servant of the Lord

Bridge terminology

Hebrew word *asham*

"Pierced through"

Punishment was on Him

Grace and restoration

We are the guilty ones

WALKING IN THE DAYLIGHT

Discussion Time

———— DISCOVER GOD'S WORD ————
Discussion/Application Questions

1. Where do we see the language of ancient Israel's sacrificial system in Isaiah 52:13–53:12?

2. What does this language tell us about God? What does it say about the servant?

3. Exodus 24 demonstrates how the sprinkling of blood was involved when God made a covenant with the people of Israel at Mount Sinai. Read Exodus 24:1–8.

   How does this passage illustrate the meaning of how the servant will "sprinkle many nations," according to Isaiah 52:15?

4. Another occasion in which the blood of sacrifice was crucial was the annual Day of Atonement. Read Leviticus 16:3–19.

How do we see what is called "substitutionary atonement"—an innocent victim suffering on behalf of a guilty party—in both the Day of Atonement and Isaiah 52:13–53:12?

5. Isaiah 53:10 refers to the servant's role as an *asham*, a guilt offering, which was the type of sacrifice that was offered in situations in which restitution for a sin was possible and thus required.

   a. What do you think is the significance of the guilt offering being applied to the servant?

   b. What does Darrell Bock mean that there is a positive element to this in that restitution provides reconnection?

6. Dr. Bock goes on to say that the servant provides not only a kind of justice through the substitution in which He takes our place, but also a restitution that restores. "This is grace. This is something that I don't deserve. I didn't earn this."

   How would you explain the concept of God's grace?

──────── BRINGING IT HOME ────────

This session ends with Michael Rydelnik and Michael Brown discussing how the servant suffers a horribly violent death and is "pierced through." We see this man suffering terribly and think, *He must be some terrible sinner!* **But we are the ones who were truly guilty. He did die for sins; but it wasn't for His sins—it was for ours.**

What is the appropriate response to such benevolence?

DAYLIGHT ON PRAYER

Spending Time with God

1. What prayer requests would you like to share with the group?

2. Conclude your prayer time by thanking God for His grace extended to you through Jesus the Messiah.

DAYLIGHT AHEAD

"Who believes our report?" Isaiah 53 begins with this question. How would that question be answered, and when? Who would make the connection between this passage and Jesus the Messiah? The disciples themselves struggled to understand it. But now we know. And now we see what Jesus was doing on our behalf when he fulfilled Isaiah 53—as the scholars reveal in Session 7 of our study.

SESSION 7

Forgiveness, Confession, and Redemption

DAYLIGHT PREVIEW

Making the Connection

Long before Jesus walked on earth in the incarnation, a Jewish prophet described a remarkable picture of a servant who would be brutally treated and would bear "our grief" and carry "our sorrows." Some have struggled to make the connection between that picture and the Man Jesus. However, this is the marvelous discovery that has touched the lives of millions who have been transformed by Jesus. Scholars Darrell Bock, Michael Brown, Walter Kaiser, and Michael Rydelnik have studied this passage in detail, and they can help us see that this connection is directed at each person— we all need what this Man of sorrows offers.

―――――――――― COME TOGETHER ――――――――――
Icebreaker Questions

1. Michael Brown mentions that he was Bar Mitzvahed when he was thirteen. Have you ever been to a Bar Mitzvah, Bat Mitzvah, or a similar rite of passage for a young person? If so, what did you find most meaningful about it?

2. Michael Brown then recounts that an even more formative thing happened to him at the age of thirteen when he saw rock music legend Jimi Hendrix in concert. What musician or group was influential to you at that stage of your life?

3. Isaiah 53 presents the concept of the servant taking the punishment for the sins of others. Can you recall either taking the rap for someone else, or someone else doing so for you?

 ## FINDING DAYLIGHT

Experience the Video

Feel free to jot down Video Notes as you watch the presentation. Use the space below for those notes.

─────────────── **VIDEO NOTES** ───────────────

Is this a personal note? That's me!

All have gone astray

Connecting to the sacrifice

Michael Brown's story about the preacher

Dead Sea Scrolls: "He shall see the light"

Darrell Bock's story about the crucifixion

The servant will be exalted

Jesus' coming: on a donkey and in the clouds

Michael Brown's story: Bar Mitzvah and Jimi Hendrix

Michael Rydelnik and forgiveness

WALKING IN THE DAYLIGHT

Discussion Time

──────────── **DISCOVER GOD'S WORD** ────────────

Discussion/Application Questions

1. Michael Rydelnik notes that when Isaiah predicted that a servant would suffer and die on behalf of Israel and the world, he understood that this was a Messianic figure, but he didn't know who that person would be. Then, in the first century, the followers of Jesus, or Yeshua, as He's called in Hebrew, eventually made the connection with Isaiah's servant.

   Read about an interaction between Jesus and His disciples in Luke 18:31–34.

   a   Why would Isaiah 53 be a natural choice for a passage Jesus had in mind?

   b. Why do you think Jesus' disciples couldn't make that kind of connection till later?

2. What does Darrell Bock mean that we have to "connect to the sacrifice" in order to benefit from it?

3. Michael Brown states, "We Jews have suffered through the centuries. But often we've suffered because of our own sins. We went into exile with Babylon and Assyria because of our own sins. That's what our Hebrew Bible tells us in texts like 2 Kings 17 and 2 Chronicles 36."

How is that different from Jesus' suffering, both in its cause and its effect?

4. Dr. Rydelnik points out that Isaiah 53:10 claims that after the servant dies He will "prolong His days"—which clearly seems to refer to the servant's resurrection from the dead. Dr. Rydelnik then notes an interesting situation in Isaiah 53:11. The footnotes in many Bible translations show that whereas the standard Hebrew text (called the Masoretic Text) for this verse reads, "He shall see and be satisfied," an ancient Isaiah scroll found in the Dead Sea Scrolls says, "He shall see the light."

What would be the significance of saying this one who dies and goes into the darkness of the grave "shall see the light"?

5. Dr. Bock recounts that one time he was giving a lecture on the historical Jesus, and during the question time that came afterward he was asked, "Isn't God asking His Son to commit suicide? And isn't that immoral for Him to die on our behalf?"

How would you answer that question?

6. Dr. Brown notes that this passage in Isaiah says the servant will be highly exalted, but first He will suffer, die, and rise. And then we have some texts that tell us the Messiah will come in meekness, while

other texts speak of an exalted Messiah. Read Zechariah 9:9 and Daniel 7:13–14.

How can both passages be true? How can the Messiah come both in humility and in power?

─────────────── BRINGING IT HOME ───────────────

1. Michael Brown observes how amazing it is that more than any other text in the Hebrew Scriptures, Isaiah 53 has been read by Jewish persons who realize, "That's me. That's Jesus." Michael Rydelnik adds that this pertains not just to Jewish people but to every person: "That's me. I was like one of those sheep that strayed, but now I believe in the Lord."

Can you relate to that type of "aha" experience?

2. Dr. Brown recalls a time when he was a fairly new follower of Jesus and a man came to his congregation and preached a message about the crucifixion. "As he was talking about the sufferings involved with crucifixion, I wanted to stop him from preaching. 'No, I deserve it! I deserve the penalty! Don't do it for me. I'm not worth it!' I was overwhelmed by the depth and passion and intensity of God's love."

How overwhelming to you is the depth and passion and intensity of God's love?

DAYLIGHT ON PRAYER

Spending Time with God

1. What burdens for yourself or others would you like the group to bring before the Lord in prayer?

2. Michael Brown points out that while we may wonder why God lets us suffer and why there is so much pain, God doesn't stand on the sidelines—but suffers with us. As you pray, ask God to come near you with His comforting presence.

DAYLIGHT AHEAD

Michael Rydelnik begins with a surprising statement as the scholars sit down for Session 8: "I believe I was the least likely person ever to come to believe in Yeshua." He, like Michael Brown and Darrell Bock, were Jewish by birth—and Jesus was not for their people. And, as Dr. Brown related, he had no idea what this saying, "Jesus Saves" was supposed to mean. Journey along with these men as they take the pathway that led them to recognizing that the man of Isaiah 53 was indeed their Savior Jesus.

Did Jesus Claim to Fulfill Isaiah 53?

DAYLIGHT PREVIEW

Jews and Jesus

Three young boys—all of Jewish birth—grow up to become Christian scholars. How can this be? What transpired in the hearts and minds of Darrell Bock, Michael Rydelnik, and Michael Brown to lead them to declare that Jesus Christ is the Messiah spoken of in Isaiah 53? And what evidence can they uncover to show that Jesus himself asserted that He was that "tender plant" of Isaiah 53:2? As scholars, these men depend on the evidence before them, which they carefully lay out to support their conviction about Jesus Christ as their Savior.

COME TOGETHER

Icebreaker Questions

1. Michael Rydelnik states, "I believe I was the least likely person ever to come to believe in Yeshua, because I was raised with the idea that Jesus was for them, and we're us. They're them, and He's not for us." Were you raised with an "us vs. them" mindset in some way?

2. Darrell Bock's parents were Jewish, but they left Judaism before he was born, resulting in isolation from the rest of the family. Has anyone in your family made a major change in religion? Did it also result in isolation?

3. Just before the end of this video, Walter Kaiser makes a comment about the Jewish educational institution for children known as *yeshiva*. What was the extent of your religious education when you were growing up?

 FINDING DAYLIGHT

Experience the Video

Feel free to jot down Video Notes as you watch the presentation. Use the space below for those notes.

───────────── VIDEO NOTES ─────────────

A remarkable passage

Michael Rydelnik, Jesus, and Isaiah 53

Jewish boys and Jesus

Darrell Bock

Michael Brown

Does Jesus claim to fulfill Isaiah 53?

    Last Supper

    Jesus in the synagogue

    Jesus at the crucifixion

Jesus' death as an innocent fulfills Isaiah 53

Did Jesus think of himself as the Messiah?

If numerous texts are denied

Luke 24: Two resurrection appearances

WALKING IN THE DAYLIGHT

Discussion Time

─────────────── DISCOVER GOD'S WORD ───────────────

Discussion/Application Questions

1. Michael Rydelnik grew up predisposed against believing in Yeshua, or Jesus, because he was raised with the idea that (1) Jesus was for "them," not for "us"; (2) Jesus didn't really fulfill any of the alleged predictions about Him in the Jewish Scriptures; (3) anyone who would believe in Jesus really would be a betrayer of the Jewish people.

    How do you think these strong predispositions came to exist?

2. Although Darrell Bock shares Dr. Rydelnik's Jewish heritage, his story is quite different. His parents left Judaism before he was born, and he grew up in a liberal Christian church in which believing in Jesus' resurrection was an option and the implied message was, "As long as you believe something and try to be moral, that's really what life is all about."

    How do you think this predisposition that Jesus and the Old Testament aren't very relevant, other than as a way to relate to God on an ethical level, came to exist?

3. **Dr. Bock notes that the Last Supper is kind of like Jesus' "last will and testament" time with His disciples. In it He said things to them that He knew they would remember. Read Luke 22:7–20.**

How do you see Jesus taking the imagery of both the Passover and Isaiah 53 and relating it to himself?

4. **Later during the Last Supper, Jesus stated, as recorded in Luke 22:37, that He was about to be arrested as a criminal in fulfillment of Isaiah 53:12. What does the fact that Jesus quoted Isaiah 53 say about how He saw himself in relation to this prophetic passage?**

5. **Take a look at an earlier story from Jesus' life. Read Luke 4:14–21. Jesus reads from Isaiah 61:1–2, which clearly seems to be related to the other passages in the book of Isaiah about the Messianic servant.**

What does this say about how Jesus saw himself?

6. **In the last chapter of the book of Luke, the risen Jesus is recorded as appearing to two disciples on the road to Emmaus and then to a larger group of His followers in Jerusalem. Read Luke 24:13–47.**

   a. **What do you think the chances are that Isaiah 53 was one of the passages Jesus was opening His disciples' minds to understand (see v. 27 and vv. 44–45)?**

b.   Why do you suppose they hadn't been able to understand until now that the Messiah had to suffer and then be resurrected and glorified (see v. 26 and v. 46)?

—————————— BRINGING IT HOME ——————————

How about you—have you been "slow of heart" to believe everything the Scriptures claim about Jesus (see Luke 24:25)? And even if you believe it in your mind, how quick are you to believe it wholeheartedly and live accordingly?

DAYLIGHT ON PRAYER

Spending Time with God

1.   We all need to be open to God's Word and its truths, and we need to strive to believe God's truth and live it out. Perhaps the group can pray for these needs to be reality in all of our lives.

2.   What prayer requests would you like to share with your group?

DAYLIGHT AHEAD

Any good argument not only presents the evidence to support the argument but it also refutes the opposing side's arguments. That's how Session 9 begins as Michael Brown notes the objections people have raised to having Jesus be the subject of Isaiah 53. From there, the panel continues to pursue other lines of evidence—for instance, did those who know Jesus recognize Him as the Messiah? Interestingly, many of the first people who began to recognize Jesus' messiahship were Jewish men and women. These are among the important observations of the final session of our study.

Final Arguments

DAYLIGHT PREVIEW

Changed Lives

The process of knowing facts and proving points is all fine and good. Nobody wants to go into an argument unprepared at the beginning and defeated at the end. But this is a topic that moves far beyond the level of debating for the sake of winning points. As Michael Rydelnik says, "This was my sin" being discussed here. This was "my sin that needed to be paid for." That changed everything for him. And indeed, recognizing that Jesus loved every man and woman enough to die a sacrificial death is the crux of the whole matter. Winning a debate may be important—but trusting a Savior truly is the most important thing of all. Changed lives. That's what Isaiah 53 is about.

COME TOGETHER

Icebreaker Questions

1. This session begins by looking at arguments that have been raised to say that Jesus could not have fulfilled the predictions in Isaiah 53. How much did you like to argue when you were a kid?

2. Michael Brown recounts a story from Acts 8 in which Philip explains to an Ethiopian official what the official is reading in Isaiah 53. Name a person who has been a blessing to you by being able to teach you or explain things to you.

3. In talking about a priestly Messiah, Dr. Brown notes that priests stand between the people and God. Who comes to your mind as a person who has played a key role in your relationship with God?

 FINDING DAYLIGHT

Experience the Video

Feel free to jot down Video Notes as you watch the presentation. Use the space below for those notes.

———————————————— VIDEO NOTES ————————————————

Arguments against Jesus as the Messiah

Did the apostles realize Jesus was the Messiah?

Not a new interpretation: Jewish teachings

The details from Isaiah 53: Fulfilled

Michael Rydelnik: Special words of Isaiah 53

"All we like sheep have gone astray; . . . but the Lord laid on him the iniquity of us all."

Darrell Bock: The resurrection

A life-changing chapter

Jesus: The fulfillment

 WALKING IN THE DAYLIGHT

Discussion Time

DISCOVER GOD'S WORD

Discussion/Application Questions

1. As this study comes to an end, read Isaiah 52:13–53:12 again.
    This session begins with a discussion of arguments that have been raised against Jesus being the Messiah. How would you respond to each of the following?

    *   Isaiah 53:3 says that the servant "was despised and rejected," yet Jesus was followed by great crowds.

- Isaiah 53:7 says that the servant "opened not His mouth," yet Jesus cried out on the cross and in various settings.

- Isaiah 53:9 says that the servant "had done no violence," yet Jesus drove the money changers out with a whip.

- Isaiah 53:10 says that the servant will "see His seed," yet Jesus didn't have offspring.

2. **When Michael Rydelnik asks if the apostles identified Jesus as the Messiah, Michael Brown refers to a passage in Matthew 8. Read Matthew 8:14–17.**

   Quoting Isaiah 53:4, how did Matthew see Jesus fulfilling this prophecy?

3. **Dr. Brown also recounts a story in the book of Acts involving Philip, a disciple of the disciples. Read Acts 8:26–39.**

   How does this story underscore the fact that the first Christians identified Jesus as the Messiah and as the fulfillment of Isaiah 53?

4. What do you think of Dr. Rydelnik's testimony to his Jewish relatives that if Jesus had been accepted by Israel, by the leaders, it would have been proof that Jesus is not the Messiah—because the Messiah has to be despised and rejected?

5. Read about the circumstances of Jesus' burial in Matthew 27:57–60.

   How do those circumstances fulfill Isaiah 53:9?

6. What is the significance of the fact that the first witnesses to Jesus' resurrection were women?

BRINGING IT HOME

1. How do you react to Michael Rydelnik's observation that the special significance of Isaiah 53 goes beyond addressing the question of whether Jesus was the Messiah and speaks to why it matters—i.e., that it was *his sin* that needed atoning, that needed forgiveness, that needed to be paid for?

2. Michael Brown reflects on how Jesus' disciples felt after He died. They were discouraged. They were ready to quit. They were fearful. They weren't expecting Jesus' resurrection, so they didn't believe it

when they heard the reports. But then Jesus opened their eyes, and they realized, "Hey, it happened! He rose from the dead!"

Then, in regard to Isaiah 53, Dr. Brown states, "It's one of these experiences which, amazingly, many people have had, Jew and Gentile, reading this text, when the light goes on and they think, *My God, this is real!*"

How would you describe your experience in exploring Isaiah 53 during this study? Have any "lights" come on?

 ## DAYLIGHT ON PRAYER

Spending Time with God

1. Has your life been changed by reflecting on Isaiah 53? Are there ways that the group can pray for your life to change more?

2. What have you appreciated the most about this group? How can the group continue to support you in prayer?